How Do Large Language Models Work? A

Beginner's Guide to AI Chatbots and Text

Generation

Table of Contents

Part 1: Introduction to Large Language Models (LLMs)

Chapter 1: What are Large Language Models?

1.1 The Power of Text: Understanding

Natural Language Processing (NLP)

Imagine a world where computers understand human language as well as we do. They can read and comprehend complex texts, translate languages seamlessly, and even hold engaging conversations. This dream, once relegated to science fiction, is becoming a reality thanks to a branch of Artificial Intelligence (AI) called Natural Language Processing (NLP).

NLP focuses on enabling computers to interact with and understand human language. It encompasses various tasks, such as:

- **Machine Translation:** Breaking down language barriers by translating text from one language to another.

- **Sentiment Analysis:** Identifying the emotional tone of a piece of text, like positive or negative sentiment in a product review.

- **Speech Recognition:** Converting spoken language into understandable text.

- **Text Summarization:** Condensing large amounts of text into a concise and informative summary.

- **Question Answering:** Extracting relevant answers to user queries from a vast amount of data.

Large Language Models (LLMs) are a powerful subfield within NLP, pushing the boundaries of what computers can achieve with language. They are essentially complex algorithms trained on massive amounts of text data, allowing them to perform a wide range of NLP tasks with remarkable accuracy.

1.2 From Simple to Superhuman: A Brief History of Language Models

The history of language models is a fascinating journey that traces back to the early days of AI research. In the 1950s, researchers began experimenting with statistical methods to predict the next word in a sequence. These early models were rudimentary, relying on simple word probabilities.

Over the next few decades, advancements in computational power and machine learning techniques led to the development of more sophisticated models. Recurrent Neural Networks (RNNs) emerged as a powerful tool for modeling sequential data like language. RNNs allowed models to learn long-term dependencies within sentences, improving their ability to capture the context of the text.

However, the real breakthrough came with the introduction of Transformer architecture in 2017. This revolutionary approach revolutionized the field by allowing models to efficiently analyze relationships between words across long distances within a sentence. This capability significantly improved a model's ability to understand the nuanced meaning of text.

1.3 What Makes Them Large? The Scale of LLM Training Data

One of the defining characteristics of LLMs is the sheer scale of data they are trained on. These models devour massive amounts of text data, including books, articles, code, and even online conversations. This allows them to build a vast internal representation of language, encompassing vocabulary, grammar rules, and even the stylistic nuances of different writing genres.

Training an LLM is a computationally intensive process. It requires powerful computers and specialized hardware like GPUs (Graphics Processing Units) to accelerate the calculations. The more data an LLM is trained on, the more sophisticated its understanding of language becomes. This is why LLMs are constantly evolving as the amount of available text data continues to grow exponentially.

However, the sheer size of LLM training data also presents challenges. Large datasets may contain biases and inaccuracies that the model can inadvertently learn and perpetuate. Addressing these issues is an ongoing area of research in the field of NLP.

This chapter has laid the foundation for our exploration of LLMs. In the next chapter, we will delve into the core idea behind LLMs -

statistical learning - and explore the building

blocks that make these models tick.

Chapter 2: The Core Idea: Statistical Learning Behind LLMs

2.1 Words as Numbers: Embeddings and Representing Language

Imagine trying to teach a computer to understand language without any concept of words themselves. It seems like an insurmountable task! This is where the concept of embeddings comes in.

Embeddings are a way to represent words as

numerical vectors, essentially translating words from the human-readable format into a language that computers can understand.

Think of an embedding as a unique address assigned to each word in a vast vocabulary. These addresses capture not only the individual meaning of a word but also its relationship to other words. Words with similar meanings will have embeddings that are closer together in this numerical space. For example, the embeddings for "happy" and "joyful" would likely be closer than the embeddings for "happy" and "sad."

There are various techniques for creating word embeddings. One popular method is word2vec, which analyzes large text corpora to identify statistical relationships between words. By analyzing how often words appear together in a sentence or paragraph, word2vec can learn the semantic meaning and context of each word.

Embeddings play a crucial role in LLM functionality. They provide a foundation for the model to understand the relationships

between words, analyze sentence structure,

and ultimately, generate human-like text.

2.2 Neural Networks for Language: The Building Blocks of LLMs

Neural networks are the workhorses behind

LLMs. These complex algorithms are loosely

inspired by the structure of the human brain

and are adept at learning complex patterns

from data. They consist of interconnected

layers of artificial neurons, which process

information and transmit signals to other

neurons in the network.

In the context of LLMs, neural networks are

specifically designed to handle language

tasks. These networks are trained on massive

amounts of text data, allowing them to learn

the statistical relationships between words

and sentences. Over time, the network

adjusts the weights and connections

between its neurons, gradually improving its

ability to understand and process language.

There are different types of neural networks used in LLMs, but a common architecture is the Recurrent Neural Network (RNN). RNNs are particularly well-suited for language tasks because they can process information sequentially. This allows them to consider the context of previous words in a sentence when predicting the next word.

2.3 The Workhorse of LLMs: Transformer Architecture Explained

While RNNs were a significant breakthrough, they had limitations in handling long-range dependencies within sentences. This is where the Transformer architecture comes in. Introduced in 2017, the Transformer revolutionized the field of NLP by offering a more efficient way to analyze relationships between words across long distances.

Unlike RNNs, which process information sequentially, the Transformer architecture employs a parallel approach. It analyzes all the words in a sentence simultaneously, allowing it to capture long-range dependencies more effectively. This parallel processing capability makes Transformers significantly faster and more efficient at understanding complex sentence structures.

The Transformer architecture relies on two key mechanisms:

- **Self-attention:** This mechanism allows the model to focus on specific parts of the input sentence that are most relevant to the current word being processed. By attending to relevant words, the model can better understand the context and generate more accurate predictions.

- **Encoder-decoder architecture:** This is a common structure in NLP tasks where the encoder processes the input sentence and the decoder generates the output. In the context of LLMs, the encoder analyzes the input text, capturing its meaning and relationships between words. The decoder then utilizes this encoded information to generate the desired output, such as a new sentence or a response to a question.

The combination of self-attention and encoder-decoder architecture makes Transformers incredibly powerful for language processing tasks. They have become the dominant architecture for training LLMs, enabling these models to achieve remarkable accuracy and fluency in their outputs.

This chapter has explored the core concepts behind LLMs, from word embeddings to neural networks and the transformative power of the Transformer architecture. With this foundation, we can now delve deeper into the training process of LLMs and explore how these models are fine-tuned to perform specific tasks.

Chapter 3: Data, Data Everywhere: Curating the Food for LLM Growth

LLMs are data-hungry beasts. Their remarkable abilities stem from their training on massive amounts of text data. But not just any text will do! Curating the right kind of data is crucial for fostering a robust and well-rounded understanding of language.

Here, we'll explore some of the key techniques used to train LLMs:

3.1 Text Classification: Teaching the Model to Categorize Information

Imagine feeding a child a steady diet of only candy. While they might develop a fondness for sweets, their overall understanding of nutrition would be skewed. Similarly, LLMs need a balanced diet of different text types.

One common training technique is text classification. Here, the LLM is presented with labeled text data, where each piece of text belongs to a specific category. Examples might include classifying news articles as "sports," "politics," or "entertainment." By analyzing the content and identifying patterns in each category, the LLM learns to distinguish different writing styles and thematic elements.

3.2 Masked Language Modeling: Predicting the Unseen Words

Think of a game where someone reads a sentence with a word missing, and you have to guess the missing word. This is essentially the idea behind masked language modeling. Here, the LLM is presented with a sentence where some words are randomly masked out. The model's task is to predict the most likely word to fill the gap based on the context of the surrounding words.

This technique helps the LLM develop a deep understanding of the relationships between words and how they function within a sentence. By constantly predicting the missing words, the model learns to analyze sentence structure, semantics, and even grammar rules.

3.3 Supervised Learning: Fine-tuning the LLM for Specific Tasks

Imagine training a dog to fetch a specific toy. Supervised learning works similarly for LLMs. In this approach, the LLM is trained on labeled data specifically designed for the task it needs to perform. For example, if the goal is to train an LLM for question answering, the data might consist of pairs of questions and corresponding answers.

By analyzing these pairs, the LLM learns to identify the key information in a question, search its internal knowledge base for relevant answers, and generate a concise and informative response. Supervised learning allows for fine-tuning the LLM for a wide range of specific tasks, making it a tremendously versatile tool.

Chapter 4: Training Challenges and Nuances

LLM training is a complex process with its

own set of challenges. Here, we'll delve into

some of the hurdles researchers face in developing these powerful models:

4.1 Overfitting and Underfitting: Finding the Training Sweet Spot

Imagine a student who memorizes every fact from a textbook but fails to grasp the underlying concepts. This is akin to overfitting in LLM training. Overfitting occurs when the model becomes too focused on the specific training data and loses its ability to generalize to unseen examples. It may perform exceptionally well on the training data but struggle with new information.

On the other hand, underfitting is like a student who hasn't studied enough. The model fails to learn the underlying patterns in the data and performs poorly on both the training data and new tasks.

Finding the sweet spot between overfitting and underfitting is an ongoing challenge. Researchers employ techniques like dropout regularization, which randomly drops out neurons during training, to prevent models from becoming overly reliant on specific data points.

4.2 Bias in Training Data: The Ethical Considerations of LLM Development

Just like humans, LLMs can inherit biases from the data they are trained on. If the training data is skewed towards a particular viewpoint or contains discriminatory language, the LLM may unknowingly perpetuate those biases in its outputs. This raises significant ethical concerns.

Mitigating bias in LLMs requires careful data curation and selection. Researchers strive to use diverse and balanced datasets that represent a variety of perspectives. Additionally, techniques like fairness-aware training algorithms are being developed to identify and address potential biases within the model itself.

4.3 Lifelong Learning: Keeping the LLM Up-to-Date

The world of language is constantly evolving. New words emerge, slang terms become mainstream, and societal trends shift. To remain relevant, LLMs need to be able to adapt and learn throughout their lifespan.

This concept of lifelong learning is an active area of research. Techniques like continual learning and online learning are being explored to enable LLMs to continuously update their knowledge base and adapt to changing language patterns.

Chapter 5: Generating Text: From Chatbots to Creative Writing

Imagine a game of Mad Libs, where you fill in the blanks of a story with random words. LLMs take a similar approach to text generation, but with a much more sophisticated understanding of language.

Here's how it works:

1. **Starting Point:** The LLM is provided with a starting prompt, which could be a single word, a sentence, or even a paragraph. This prompt sets the context for the text generation process.

2. **Predicting the Next Word:** Based on the prompt and its internal knowledge of language patterns, the LLM predicts the most likely word to follow. It considers factors like the surrounding words, grammar rules, and the overall thematic flow.

3. **Building the Sequence:** The predicted word is then added to the existing text, and the process repeats. The LLM continues to predict the next most likely

word, building a sequence that adheres to the established context and style.

4. **Controlling the Output:** Different techniques can be employed to control the direction and style of the generated text. For instance, temperature control can influence the randomness of the generated text. A higher temperature leads to more creative and surprising outputs, while a lower temperature results in more predictable and safer text.

5.2 Beyond Prediction: Creativity and Style in LLM Text Generation

LLMs are not simply sophisticated Mad Libs machines. They can exhibit a surprising degree of creativity in their text generation. By analyzing vast amounts of creative writing data, LLMs can learn to mimic different writing styles, generate different creative text formats like poems or code, and even craft narratives with plot and character development.

However, it's important to remember that LLMs are not sentient beings. Their creativity is based on statistical patterns and associations learned from data. They can generate seemingly creative text, but they may not possess a deep understanding of the meaning or intent behind their creations.

5.3 The Future of Content Creation: LLMs as Co-authors and Storytellers

The ability of LLMs to generate human-quality text has significant implications for the future of content creation. Here are some potential applications:

- **Co-writing with Humans:** LLMs can act as co-authors, suggesting ideas, completing sentences, or even generating different creative text formats to help human writers overcome writer's block or explore new creative avenues.

- **Personalized Content:** LLMs can personalize content based on user preferences or demographics. Imagine a news article that tailors its writing style and vocabulary to the individual reader.

- **Automated Content Generation:** LLMs can be used to generate routine content, such as product descriptions or social media posts, freeing up human writers to focus on more complex tasks.

However, ethical considerations remain. It's crucial to ensure transparency about LLM-generated content and avoid situations where AI-created text is misrepresented as human-written work.

Chapter 6: Understanding and Responding to Human Language

LLMs aren't just about generating text; they can also understand and respond to human language in meaningful ways. Here, we'll explore some of the key functionalities in this area:

6.1 Question Answering: Extracting Meaning from User Queries

Imagine a powerful research assistant that can answer your questions in a comprehensive and informative way. That's

the potential of LLMs in question answering.

These models can be trained on vast

amounts of text and code, allowing them to

extract relevant information and provide

concise answers to user queries.

This capability is particularly valuable for

applications like virtual assistants and search

engines. LLMs can go beyond simply finding

relevant web pages and delve deeper,

understanding the intent behind a question

and generating informative summaries or answers directly.

6.2 Machine Translation: Breaking Down Language Barriers

Imagine a world where language is no longer a barrier to communication. Machine translation, powered by LLMs, is making significant strides towards this goal. By analyzing massive amounts of translated text data, LLMs can learn the nuances of different languages and translate text with remarkable accuracy and fluency.

This technology has the potential to revolutionize global communication, fostering collaboration and understanding across cultures. However, challenges remain, such as capturing the subtleties of humor, sarcasm, and cultural references that can get lost in translation.

6.3 Summarization: Condensing Information While Retaining Key Points

In today's information overload, the ability to quickly grasp the essence of a lengthy text is more important than ever. LLMs can be trained to generate summaries of factual topics, news articles, or even research papers. These summaries capture the key points and essential information while condensing the original text into a more manageable format.

This capability is valuable for researchers, students, and anyone who needs to efficiently process large amounts of information. However, it's important to remember that summaries may not capture all the nuances of the original text.

Chapter 7: LLMs and the Future of Search and Information Access

LLMs are poised to revolutionize the way we search for information and access knowledge. Here's how:

7.1 Revolutionizing Search Engines: Personalization and Advanced Understanding

Search engines today rely on keyword matching, which can often lead to irrelevant results. LLMs can take search to the next level by understanding the user's intent behind a query. They can analyze the context of the search, consider the user's past behavior, and personalize search results to deliver the most relevant and useful information.

Imagine searching for "best restaurants in Paris" and getting results tailored to your specific preferences, like budget, cuisine type, or even a romantic ambiance. LLMs can make search engines more intuitive and user-friendly, leading to a more efficient and

satisfying information discovery process.

7.2 The Rise of Conversational Interfaces: Talking Directly to Machines

Imagine interacting with a virtual assistant

that can understand your natural language

and respond in a comprehensive and helpful

way. This is the promise of conversational

interfaces powered by LLMs. These

interfaces allow users to interact with

machines using spoken language or text chat,

making technology more accessible and user-friendly.

Conversational interfaces have the potential to transform various industries, from customer service to healthcare. They can provide immediate assistance, answer questions, and even complete tasks based on user instructions. However, ensuring these interfaces are unbiased, respectful, and secure remains a crucial challenge.

Chapter 8: LLMs and the Evolving World of Work

LLMs are poised to impact the workplace in significant ways, potentially changing how we work and the types of skills that are valued. Here's a closer look:

8.1 Automation and Efficiency: How LLMs Can Transform Workflows

LLMs can automate repetitive and time-consuming tasks, freeing up human workers to focus on more creative and strategic endeavors. For instance, LLMs can be used to generate reports, analyze data, or even write routine emails. This automation can increase efficiency and productivity across various industries.

However, automation also raises concerns about job displacement. It's crucial to develop strategies for workforce reskilling and upskilling to ensure a smooth transition as LLMs take on more tasks.

8.2 Human-AI Collaboration: Partnering with LLMs for Enhanced Productivity

LLMs are not meant to replace human workers, but rather to augment their capabilities. They can act as powerful collaborators, providing insights, suggesting solutions, and automating tedious tasks. Imagine a doctor using an LLM to analyze patient data and generate personalized treatment recommendations, or a writer leveraging an LLM for brainstorming ideas and overcoming writer's block.

The future of work lies in human-AI collaboration, where humans leverage the strengths of LLMs to achieve better

outcomes.

Chapter 9: Ethical Considerations and Potential Biases

The remarkable capabilities of LLMs come

with a set of ethical considerations that need

to be addressed:

9.1 Fairness and Transparency: Ensuring Responsible LLM Development

As discussed earlier, LLMs can inherit biases

from the data they are trained on. This can

lead to discriminatory or unfair outputs. It's crucial to ensure transparency in LLM development and deployment. This includes making data collection practices and model training methodologies more transparent. Additionally, fairness-aware algorithms and techniques are being developed to mitigate bias in LLM outputs.

9.2 The Future of Work: The Impact of LLMs on Jobs and Human Skills

The automation potential of LLMs raises concerns about job displacement. It's important to prepare the workforce for the changing landscape. Upskilling and reskilling initiatives will be essential to ensure that workers possess the skills necessary to thrive in an AI-powered workplace.

Furthermore, as LLMs become more sophisticated, it's important to have clear guidelines and regulations in place to govern their use. This includes addressing issues like deepfakes, misinformation, and potential misuse of LLM capabilities.

Chapter 10: Conclusion: The Potential and Promise of Large Language Models

Large Language Models represent a significant leap forward in the field of Artificial Intelligence. Their ability to understand and generate human-like language opens up a world of possibilities across various domains. From revolutionizing search engines to fostering human-AI collaboration in the workplace, LLMs have the potential to transform the way we interact with technology and information.

However, it's crucial to acknowledge the challenges and ethical considerations that come with this powerful technology. Developing and deploying LLMs responsibly, with a focus on fairness, transparency, and human well-being, will be paramount in harnessing the full potential of these groundbreaking models.

The future of LLMs is bright,but it is also a future that we must shape. By fostering collaboration between researchers, developers, policymakers, and the public, we can ensure that LLMs are used for the benefit of humanity. Here are some key areas for ongoing exploration:

- **Explainability and Interpretability:** Developing methods to understand how LLMs arrive at their outputs will be crucial for building trust and ensuring responsible use.

- **Lifelong Learning:** Enabling LLMs to continuously learn and adapt to new information will be essential for their long-term relevance and effectiveness.

- **Human-AI Partnership:** Research on how humans and LLMs can best collaborate to achieve optimal outcomes will be vital in the future workplace.

- **Societal Impact Assessments:** Proactive evaluation of the potential societal impacts of LLMs, including their influence on education, communication, and culture, will be crucial for mitigating potential risks.

LLMs represent a powerful new chapter in our relationship with technology. By approaching their development and deployment with a sense of responsibility and a commitment to human well-being, we can unlock the vast potential of these models to create a brighter future for all.

www.ingramcontent.com/pod-product-compliance
Lightning Source LLC
LaVergne TN
LVHW051611050326
832903LV00033B/4455